D1402741

**The Generation Series-
Grandpa Is A *Cubs* Fan, Daddy Is A *Cubs* Fan, I Am A *Cubs* Fan**

Text © 2010 by Stephen Davern
Photo © 2010 by Kristine Kilroy Dunne

Back cover text provided courtesy of John Maher.

*Major League Baseball trademarks and copyrights are used
with permission of Major League Baseball Properties, Inc.*

All rights reserved. No part of this publication may be reproduced
or transmitted in any form or by any means, electronic or mechanical, including
photocopy, recording, or any information storage and retrieval system, without
permission in writing from the publisher.

Requests for permission to make copies of any part of the work
should be submitted online at info@mascotbooks.com or mailed to
Mascot Books 560 Herndon Parkway #120, Herndon, VA 20170

Printed in the United States.

PRT0610A

ISBN-13: 978-1-936319-06-0
ISBN-10: 1-936319-06-3

Mascot Books
560 Herndon Parkway #120, Herndon, VA 20170

www.mascotbooks.com

Have a book idea? Contact us at:
Mascot Books
P.O. Box 220157
Chantilly, VA 20153-0157
info@mascotbooks.com

To the many generations of
loyal Chicago Cubs fans.

Special thanks to Michael and Colleen Claffey.

~Stephen Davern

Grandpa Is A Cubs™ Fan
Daddy Is A Cubs™ Fan
I Am A Cubs™ Fan

Stephen Davern

Illustrated by Brent McCarthy

Grandpa is a *Cubs* fan!

Grandpa says we are Cubs fans!

Grandpa and Daddy took
the 22 Clark bus to the
Cubs game.

Grandpa and Daddy chased home run balls sailing out of the ballpark during batting practice.

Grandpa and Daddy liked
to sit in the bleachers.

Hats off! It was time to
sing the National Anthem.

They got their pencils and scorecards ready. It was time to "Play Ball!"

Daddy liked to watch the man in the scoreboard change the numbers during the game.

"Cubs win!" they all shouted as they waved to the firemen of Engine Company 78.

Daddy liked being a Cubs fan
because the games were always
over way before bedtime.

Daddy loved going to Cubs games with Grandpa.

Daddy is a Cubs fan!

Daddy is taking me to a Cubs game today!

The **22 Clark** bus dropped us off right in front of *Wrigley Field.*

I caught a ball that was hit out of the park during batting practice.

Daddy and I sat in the same bleacher seats that he and Grandpa used to sit in.

Hats off! Time to sing the National Anthem.

Get your pencils and scorecards ready. It's time to "Play Ball!"

I like to watch the man in the scoreboard change the numbers during the game.

"Cubs Win!" we all shouted
as we waved to the firemen
of Engine Company 78.

Daddy says we can go to a Cubs game at nighttime when I get older!

I love going to Cubs
games with Daddy!

I am a Cubs fan!

Someday, I'll be a daddy and I
will take my kid to a Cubs game.

About the Author

Photo by Kristine Kilroy Dunne

Stephen "Steve" Davern loves
his family, friends, music, sports,
history, America and anything that
reminds him of his father.

For free music downloads, visit
myspace.com/stevedavern

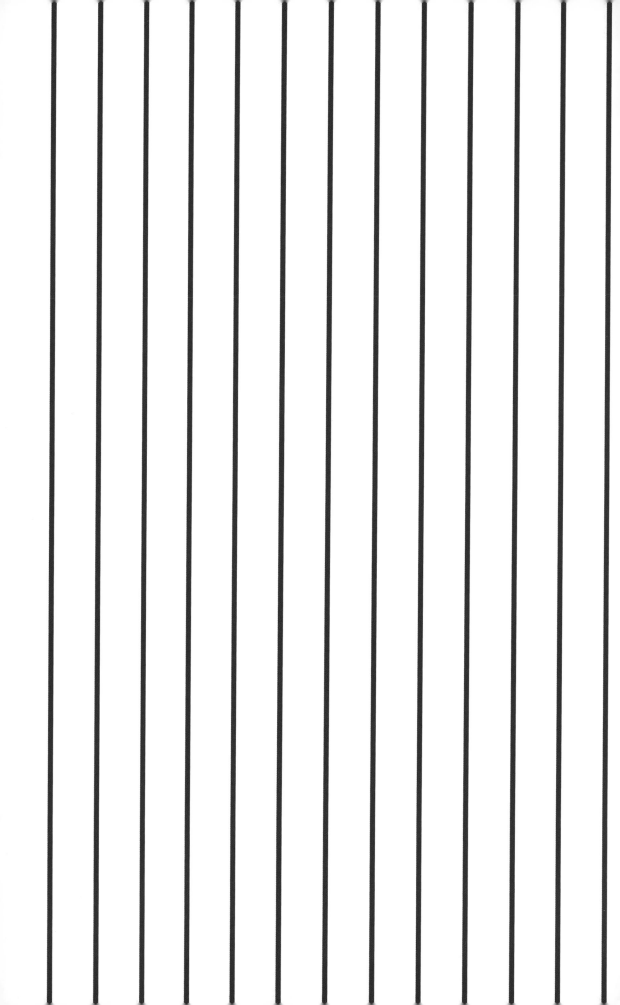

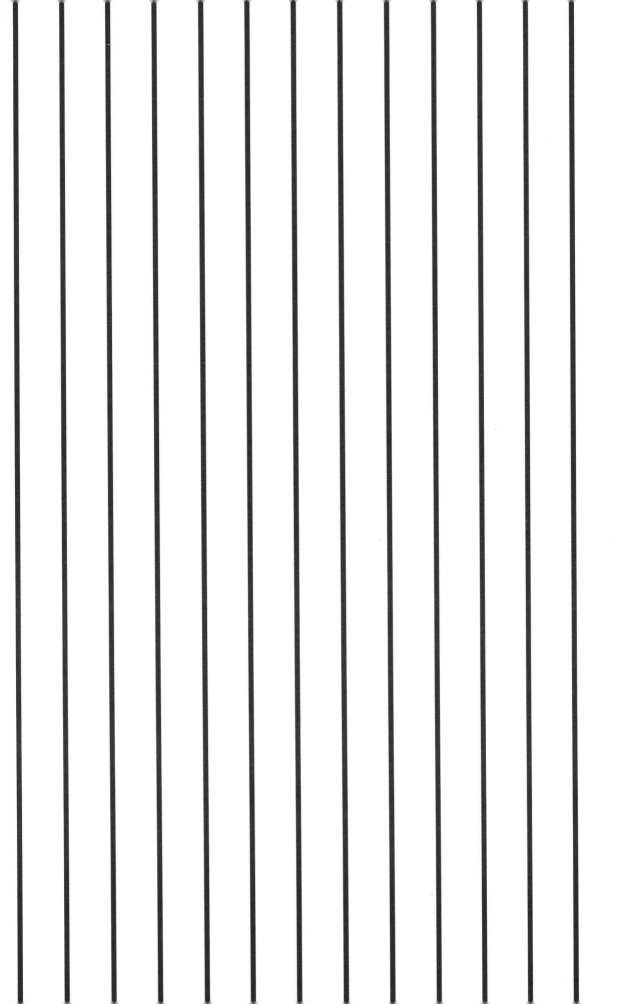

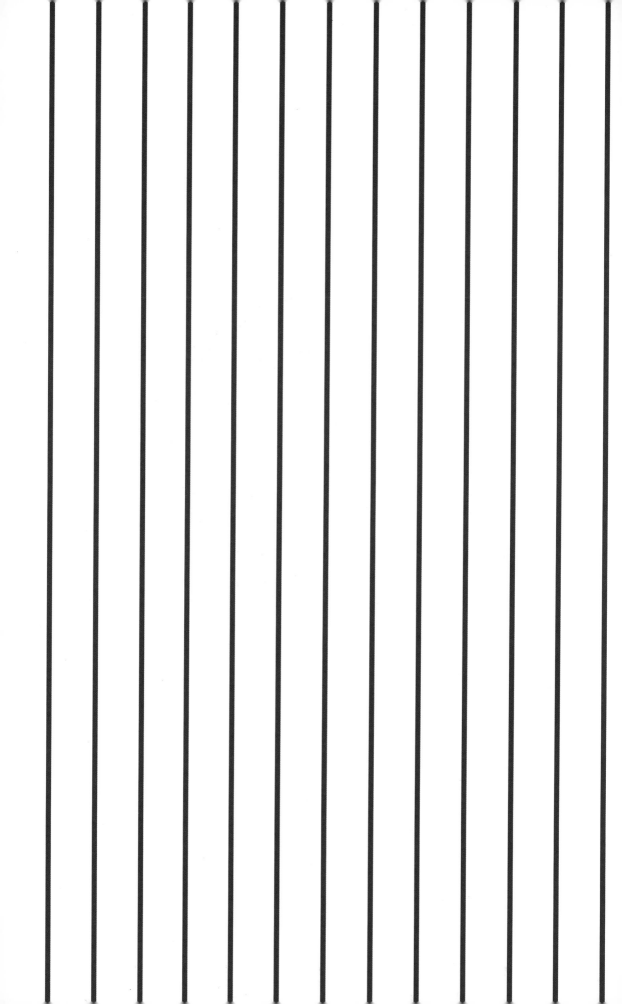